INTRODUCTION

Seashore life is distributed in a number of life zones along shorelines. Creatures living in high tide zones get wet by tides twice daily. Those in mid-tide zones are covered by water most of the time. Those in low tide zones are almost always submerged.

The best time to observe the greatest variety of species is during low tide. Tide times are often published in newspapers and online, and tide tables are available at most sporting goods stores. There are generally two tides a day, and tidal differences may be as much as 15 ft. (4.5 m). The lowest tides of the year occur in midwinter and midsummer.

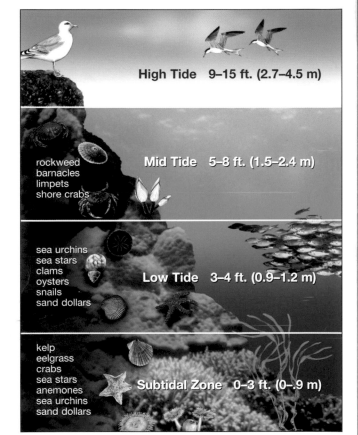

High Tide 9–15 ft. (2.7–4.5 m)

rockweed
barnacles
limpets
shore crabs

Mid Tide 5–8 ft. (1.5–2.4 m)

sea urchins
sea stars
clams
oysters
snails
sand dollars

Low Tide 3–4 ft. (0.9–1.2 m)

kelp
eelgrass
crabs
sea stars
anemones
sea urchins
sand dollars

Subtidal Zone 0–3 ft. (0–.9 m)

Most illustrations show the adult male in breeding coloration. Colors and markings may be duller or absent during different seasons. The measurements denote the length of species from nose/bill to tail tip. Illustrations are not to scale.

Waterford Press produces reference guides that introduce novices to nature, science, survival and outdoor recreation. Product information is featured on the website: www.waterfordpress.com.

To order or for information on custom published products please call 800-434-2555 or email orderdesk@waterfordpress.com.

For permissions or to share comments email editor@waterfordpress.com.

ISBN 978-1-62005-493-2

$7.95 U.S.

Made in the USA

216701

NORTHWEST SEASHORE LIFE

NORTHWEST SEASHORE LIFE – A Waterproof Folding Guide to Familiar Animals & Plants — Kavanagh/Leung

A Waterproof Folding Guide to Familiar Animals & Plants

T0124024

SEASHORE PLANTS

Rockweed
Fucus spp.
To 20 in. (50 cm)
Ribbed stem is covered with swollen air bladders.

Eelgrass
Zostera marina
To 4 ft. (1.2 m)

Sea Sack
Halosaccion glandiforme
To 4 in. (10 cm)

Surf Grass
Phyllospadix spp.
Blades to 6 ft. (1.8 m) long

Sea Palm
Postelsia palmaeformis
To 2 ft. (60 cm)

Bull Kelp
Nereocystis luetkeana
To 65 ft. (20 m) long
Long blades radiate from a single float.

Giant Kelp
Macrocystis spp.
Blades to 30 in. (75 cm)
Each blade is attached to a round float.

Sea Lettuce
Ulva lactuca
To 26 in. (65 cm)

Beach Pea
Lathyrus japonicus
To 2 ft. (60 cm)
Creeping plant found on dunes and beaches.

Beach Morning Glory
Calystegia soldanella
To 6 in. (15 cm) tall
Creeping plant.

Yellow Sand Verbena
Abronia latifolia
To 6 in. (15 cm)

Beach Strawberry
Fragaria chiloensis
To 8 in. (20 cm)

California Poppy
Eschscholzia californica californica
To 2 ft. (60 cm)
Leaves are fern-like.

Dune Tansy
Tanacetum camphoratum
To 2 ft. (60 cm)

SEA STARS, ANEMONES & ALLIES

Sea Pen
Ptilosarcus gurneyi
To 18 in. (45 cm)

Daisy Brittle Star
Ophiopholis aculeata
To 9 in. (23 cm)

Spiny Sun Star
Crossaster papposus
To 14 in. (35 cm)

Ochre Sea Star
Pisaster ochraceus
To 20 in. (50 cm)
May be red, purple, orange or brown.

Bat Star
Patiria miniata
To 8 in. (20 cm)
May be red-brown to reddish.

Brooding Anemone
Epiactis prolifera
To 1.5 in. (4 cm)

Purple Sea Urchin
Strongylocentrotus purpuratus
To 4 in. (10 cm)

Giant Green Anemone
Anthopleura xanthogrammica
To 12 in. (30 cm)

Aggregate Anemone
Anthopleura elegantissima
To 20 in. (50 cm)
Usually grow in clumps.

Green Sea Urchin
Strongylocentrotus droebachiensis
To 3 in. (8 cm)

Moon Jellyfish
Aurelia aurita
To 16 in. (40 cm)
Commonly washed up on beaches after storms.

Frilled Anemone
Metridium senile
To 18 in. (45 cm)

Sand Dollar
Dendraster excentricus
To 3 in. (8 cm)

Lion's Mane Jellyfish
Cyanea capillata
To 8 ft. (2.4 m)
Note large size.

By-the-wind Sailor
Velella velella
To 3 in. (8 cm)
Small crest on upper surface acts as a sail.

MOLLUSKS

Rough Keyhole Limpet
Diodora aspera
To 3 in. (8 cm)

Black Turban Snail
Tegula funebralis
To 1 in. (3 cm)

Pacific Littleneck Clam
Protothaca staminea
To 3 in. (8 cm)

Blue Mussel
Mytilus edulis
To 4 in. (10 cm)
Grows attached to pilings and other marine objects.

Purple Dwarf Olive
Olivella biplicata
To 1.25 in. (3.6 cm)

Frilled Dogwinkle
Nucella lamellosa
To 3 in. (8 cm)

California Mussel
Mytilus californianus
To 10 in. (25 cm)
Shell has prominent ridges.

Lined Chiton
Tonicella lineata
To 2 in. (5 cm)

Eroded Periwinkle
Littorina keenae
To .75 in. (2 cm)

Northern Abalone
Haliotis kamtschatkana
To 6 in. (15 cm)

Giant Western Nassa
Nassarius fossatus
To 2 in. (5 cm)

Heart Cockle
Clinocardium nuttallii
To 6 in. (15 cm)

Giant Pacific Oyster
Crassostrea gigas
To 12 in. (30 cm)

Giant Pacific Scallop
Patinopecten caurinus
To 10 in. (25 cm)

Pacific Pink Scallop
Chlamys hastata
To 3 in. (8 cm)

Pacific Razor Clam
Siliqua patula
To 7 in. (18 cm)

MOLLUSKS

Geoduck
Panopea abrupta To 9 in. (23 cm)
The largest burrowing clam in the world.

Horse Mussel
Modiolus modiolus
To 6 in. (15 cm)

Soft-shelled Clam
Mya arenaria
To 6 in. (15 cm)

CRUSTACEANS & ALLIES

Hermit Crab
Pagurus spp.
To 1.3 in. (3.6 cm)
Lives in discarded snail shells.

Dungeness Crab
Cancer magister
To 9 in. (23 cm)

Purple Shore Crab
Hemigrapsus nudus
To 2.5 in. (6 cm)

Gooseneck Barnacle
Lepas anatifera
To 6 in. (15 cm)
Often found attached to floating objects.

Porcelain Crab
Petrolisthes cinctipes
To 1 in. (3 cm)
Very common along rocky shorelines under stones.

Coon-striped Shrimp
Pandalus danae
To 6 in. (15 cm)

Mole Crab
Emerita spp.
To 1.5 in. (4 cm)
Moves in and out with the tide on open beaches.

Barnacle
Balanus spp.
To 3 in. (8 cm)
Grows in clusters on rocks and piers.

Red Crab
Cancer productus
To 6 in. (15 cm)

BEACH DRIFT

Sea Urchin Skeleton

Dogfish Egg Case

Skate Egg Case

Sand Dollar Skeleton

Bay Pipefish
Syngnathus leptorhynchus
To 14 in. (35 cm)

Sculpin
Family Cottidae To 30 in. (75 cm)
Several dozen species are found in shallow water and tidepools.

Kelp Greenling
Hexagrammos decagrammus
To 20 in. (50 cm)
Dark males have blue spots.

Eulachon
Thaleichthys pacificus To 10 in. (25 cm)

Pacific Herring
Clupea pallasii To 18 in. (45 cm)

Northern Anchovy
Engraulis mordax To 9 in. (23 cm)

Yelloweye Rockfish
Sebastes ruberrimus
To 3 ft. (90 cm)

Copper Rockfish
Sebastes caurinus To 22 in. (55 cm)

China Rockfish
Sebastes nebulosus To 17 in. (43 cm)

Striped Seaperch
Embiotoca lateralis To 15 in. (38 cm)

Lingcod
Ophiodon elongatus To 5 ft. (1.5 m)

Striped Bass
Morone saxatilis To 6 ft. (1.8 m)
Has 6–9 dark side stripes.

Chinook (King) Salmon
Oncorhynchus tshawytscha To 5 ft. (1.5 m)
Has dark spots on back and tail. Gums are black at tooth base. The largest salmon.

Spiny Dogfish
Squalus acanthias To 5 ft. (1.5 m)

Walleye Pollock
Theragra chalcogramma
To 3 ft. (90 cm)

Coho (Silver) Salmon
Oncorhynchus kisutch To 40 in. (1 m)
Has white gums and a black tongue. Breeding male has red side stripes.

Common Loon
Gavia immer To 3 ft. (90 cm)

Winter
Summer

Red-throated Loon
Gavia stellata To 25 in. (63 cm)

Pied-billed Grebe
Podilymbus podiceps
To 13 in. (33 cm)
Note banded white bill.

Horned Grebe
Podiceps auritus
To 15 in. (38 cm)
Note reddish neck and ear tufts.

Western Grebe
Aechmophorus occidentalis
To 25 in. (63 cm)

Ring-necked Duck
Aythya collaris To 18 in. (45 cm)
Note white ring near bill tip.

American Wigeon
Mareca americana To 23 in. (58 cm)

Northern Shoveler
Spatula clypeata To 20 in. (50 cm)
Named for its large spatulate bill.

Northern Pintail
Anas acuta To 29 in. (73 cm)

Canvasback
Aythya valisineria To 2 ft. (60 cm)

Mallard
Anas platyrhynchos To 28 in. (70 cm)

Green-winged Teal
Anas crecca To 16 in. (40 cm)

Blue-winged Teal
Spatula discors To 16 in. (40 cm)

Bufflehead
Bucephala albeola To 15 in. (38 cm)

Common Goldeneye
Bucephala clangula To 20 in. (50 cm)

Surf Scoter
Melanitta perspicillata To 20 in. (50 cm)
Note white patches on nape and forehead.

White-winged Scoter
Melanitta fusca To 23 in. (58 cm)
Note white wing patches.

Ruddy Duck
Oxyura jamaicensis To 16 in. (40 cm)

Lesser Scaup
Aythya affinis To 18 in. (45 cm)
Note peaked crown.

Double-crested Cormorant
Phalacrocorax auritus
To 3 ft. (90 cm)

Common Merganser
Mergus merganser To 27 in. (68 cm)

Tundra Swan
Cygnus columbianus
To 4.5 ft. (1.4 m)

American Coot
Fulica americana To 16 in. (40 cm)

Canada Goose
Branta canadensis
To 45 in. (1.14 m)

Snow Goose
Chen caerulescens
To 31 in. (78 cm)

Brant
Branta bernicla
To 26 in. (65 cm)
Note white neck mark.

Sanderling
Calidris alba
To 8 in. (20 cm)
Runs in and out with waves along shorelines.

Willet
Tringa semipalmata
To 17 in. (43 cm)
Wings flash black and white in flight.

Wilson's Snipe
Gallinago delicata
To 12 in. (30 cm)

Western Sandpiper
Calidris mauri
To 7 in. (18 cm)

Least Sandpiper
Calidris minutilla
To 6 in. (15 cm)

Spotted Sandpiper
Actitis macularius
To 8 in. (20 cm)
Breast is spotted.

Black Turnstone
Arenaria melanocephala
To 9 in. (23 cm)

American Avocet
Recurvirostra americana
To 20 in. (50 cm)

Black-bellied Plover
Pluvialis squatarola
To 14 in. (35 cm)

Greater Yellowlegs
Tringa melanoleuca
To 15 in. (38 cm)
Call is a 3–5 note whistle.

Lesser Yellowlegs
Tringa flavipes
To 10 in. (25 cm)
Call is a 1–3 note whistle.

Marbled Godwit
Limosa fedoa
To 20 in. (50 cm)
Long bill is slightly upturned.

Killdeer
Charadrius vociferus
To 12 in. (30 cm)
Note two breast bands.

Semipalmated Plover
Charadrius semipalmatus
To 8 in. (20 cm)
Note single breast band.

Black Oystercatcher
Haematopus bachmani
To 18 in. (45 cm)

Black-necked Stilt
Himantopus mexicanus
To 17 in. (43 cm)

Long-billed Curlew
Numenius americanus
To 26 in. (65 cm)
Long bill is slightly downturned.

Great Blue Heron
Ardea herodias
To 4.5 ft. (1.4 m)

Tufted Puffin
Fratercula cirrhata
To 16 in. (40 cm)

Common Murre
Uria aalge
To 17 in. (43 cm)

Herring Gull
Larus argentatus
To 26 in. (65 cm)
Legs are pinkish.

Glaucous-winged Gull
Larus glaucescens
To 27 in. (68 cm)
Gray wings lack black markings. Legs are pinkish.

Ring-billed Gull
Larus delawarensis
To 20 in. (50 cm)
Bill has dark ring.

Bonaparte's Gull
Chroicocephalus philadelphia
To 14 in. (35 cm)

Belted Kingfisher
Megaceryle alcyon
To 14 in. (35 cm)

Western Gull
Larus occidentalis
To 27 in. (68 cm)
Large gull has a dark back.

American Crow
Corvus brachyrhynchos
To 22 in. (55 cm)
Call is a distinct – caw.

Bald Eagle
Haliaeetus leucocephalus
To 40 in. (1 m)

Red-winged Blackbird
Agelaius phoeniceus
To 9 in. (23 cm)

Osprey
Pandion haliaetus
To 2 ft. (60 cm)

Northern Sea Lion
Eumetopias jubatus
To 10.5 ft. (3.2 m)
Males have hairy necks.

California Sea Lion
Zalophus californianus
To 8 ft. (2.4 m)
Note domed skull.

Harbor Porpoise
Phocoena phocoena
To 6 ft. (1.8 m)

Harbor Seal
Phoca vitulina To 6 ft. (1.8 m)

Pacific White-sided Dolphin
Lagenorhynchus obliquidens
To 8 ft. (2.4 m)

Dall's Porpoise
Phocoenoides dalli
To 7 ft. (2.1 m)

Sea Otter
Enhydra lutris
To 6 ft. (1.8 m)

Common Dolphin
Delphinus delphis
To 9 ft. (2.7 m)

Killer Whale
Orcinus orca
To 30 ft. (9 m)

Humpback Whale
Megaptera novaeangliae
To 50 ft. (15 m)

Finback Whale
Balaenoptera physalus
To 80 ft. (24 m)

Gray Whale
Eschrichtius robustus
To 50 ft. (15 m)

INCHES
CM